How I Flatlined and Woke Up in 45 Days

How I Flatlined and Woke Up in 45 Days

A Guide To Empowered Living

CHERYL WOOD

How I Flatlined and Woke Up in 45 Days – A Guide To Empowered Living.

Published by Cheryl Wood
Upper Marlboro, MD
Email: info@momsrthebest.com
Websites: www.momsrthebest.com; www.momsrthebest.net

ISBN 978-1-60458-733-3

I dedicate this book to my husband, James Wood, and our three beautiful children – Jayana, James II, and Jalen – who keep me inspired and fulfilled in life.

ACKNOWLEDGEMENTS

To my mom, Joyce Swann; my sister, Chere Cofield; and my brother, Michael Swann: Having a family who is united and supportive is priceless. I love you more than words could ever express. You are my ROCK, always in my corner one-hundred percent regardless of the endeavor, goal, or pursuit, and always there to cheer me on. You are the true picture of a strong inner circle. Thank you for keeping me grounded and focused on what is priority in life.

To my late dad, David Swann (R.I.P.): I was unprepared for your sudden passing and I miss you so much. But you were a fighter and I have naturally inherited that quality from you. This book is one of the many demonstrations of the fighter within to accomplish anything I set my mind to do. I promise to keep making you proud.

To my family, friends, supporters, and network of social media connections: I could not have achieved this milestone without you. A successful entrepreneur recognizes the importance of a supportive network. You have encouraged me, inspired me, and motivated me to remain dedicated to my journey. Thank you for believing in me.

"Life is an intricately designed rollercoaster with countless twists, turns, dips, and loops. Only those who swallow their fear and face the twists, turns, dips, and loops head-on are able to build character, become stronger, and soar to higher heights…
not those who avoid the rollercoaster."

- Cheryl Wood -

contents

45-Day Guide to Empowered Living

contents

A CHANGE WITHIN

As far back as I can recall I have always viewed life as the ultimate experience. I live on the premise that no individual should exist aimlessly or without direction and purpose. Life is meant to be lived and experienced. However, somewhere along the line my lofty ideas of what life should be got lost. My belief system of purposeful living became blurred and I slipped into a state of aimlessness, void of progression and advancement – I flatlined!

While reflecting on when the initial change within occurred, I think back to the first time I experienced the feeling that I was destined for something more in my life. I realize it was at the onset of motherhood that I first experienced these feelings. At the ripe age of 30 years old, after being assured by numerous doctors that I would never have children due to years of medical complications, I received the exciting and shocking news that I was expecting my first child. My world as I had known it instantly changed. Prior to motherhood I existed with a sense of contentment about my life. Content that I worked a good job, earned a decent salary, did not have many serious responsibilities, and could make decisions about my life based on what was best for only me. But with a child on the way existing only for self was no longer an option. Regardless of how much I might attempt to ignore or distract the maternal feelings within, I did not possess the ability to escape the power and force of motherhood. At 31 years of age, my firstborn child entered the world and brought more joy and contentment to my life than I had ever experienced. I was unquestionably a new person and a changed woman.

Everything I thought I knew and thought I believed prior to motherhood changed. My thought processes were different, my choices were different, my life decisions were different, and my inner being was different. This innocent bundle of joy was now my primary focus and it became clear that the manner in which I lived my life would no longer affect only me, but would directly affect this precious child in the present and in the future. For the first time in my life, I began wanting an independence that I had never desired before. I wanted flexibility and I wanted freedom to be the best mother I could be for my child. But the question kept haunting me, "How can I be the best mother to my child if I am confined to a situation where someone else dictates my time and schedule?" From that point forward the idea of creating change in my life was born and would slowly be cultivated.

My intense desire for independence and freedom continued to grow when I was blessed with two more bundles of joy (two sons) a few years after the birth of my daughter. My desire to spend time with and be available to all three of my children presented a war within my innermost being. Although I valued having a secular job that allowed me to provide for my children's material needs, my desire to be the primary influence in their lives, to mold and shape who they would become, and to spend the quality time needed to instill high standards of morals, values, and principles in their lives far outweighed my attachment to any material possessions. I loathed the idea of having my children in someone else's care for 10-12 hours a day while I worked outside of the home. But as a mother of three, even with my husband by my side, realistically, our financial obligations took precedence and my desire to be actively involved in my children's lives seemed to fade further and further into the background. I began to feel that my desire was more of an unachievable dream rather than a potential reality. As the cycle continued, the balancing act of my life began to weigh heavily on me.

SLIPPING INTO UNCONSCIOUSNESS

The demands of being a wife, mother of three, and full-time employee outside of the home became extremely overbearing. My life had quickly accelerated from slow motion to wharp speed but it was not proceeding in the direction I desired. Every day and every activity of my life became a rush against the clock. The more I rushed, the unhappier I became as I realized I was also rushing through my children's lives. My 16-17 hour days of getting up at 5 o'clock in the morning, working 8-hours a day on a secular job, coming home to handle the household responsibilities of a mother of three, and not going to bed until 10 o'clock or later became exhausting and grueling. I began feeling empty and hollow inside as if I were nothing more than a robot or a machine programmed on autopilot. I recall many days I was so drained from the routine that after dropping off my children at school in the mornings I would sit in my car in a daze feeling that this vicious cycle would never end. It was taking a drastic toll on my mind and my body. I was spending less quality time with my family and more time stressed about how I would accomplish everything in a 24-hour period. I ceased giving my husband and children the best of me. Instead, they were getting the leftovers – the exhausted, overextended, overworked, rushed, and frantic wife and mother who was trying desperately to find balance without any progression. And, regardless of my attempts there was always some aspect of my life that I could not keep up with. My unhappiness was further driven by the fact that my lack of available time for my family forced me to make what I considered to be unfair choices – either sit at the dinner table to enjoy a meal with my family in the evening or head to the laundry room to wash and iron clothes in preparation for the next day; either spend quality time reading and playing with my children after school or make lunches and pack snack bags for the following school day; either spend quality time nurturing my relationship with my husband or go to bed at a decent hour to get enough rest to remain energized for my grueling routine. Even my weekends became a self-debate of whether to handle household chores or spend quality time with my family. There was always something that lacked the attention and focus it needed within my household. I began feeling deeply frustrated and irritated that I could not find a way out of this chaotic lifestyle. And the more I focused on how greatly I detested all the rushing, the hurrying, and the choices on how to allocate my time, I started to become sluggish and depressed. I was wide awake, yet, unconscious. I desperately desired independence, freedom, and flexibility to prioritize my life as I deemed necessary. I wanted to work hard but for myself; I wanted to set my own hours and have a flexible schedule to attend field trips and PTA meetings at my children's schools; and I wanted to experience true happiness doing something I loved and was passionate about Instead, I was taking a quick downward spiral fall and it seemed there was no way to stop it.

Before long, I completely flatlined! It was as though I was lying on a hospital bed and could see the doctor's working to revive me but with no response, no vital signs, and no heartbeat. Despite my diligent efforts to get up off the hospital bed, I could not move. I was paralyzed into inactivity, immobile, and lifeless. As I slipped deeper and deeper into this flatlined condition my focus, my drive, and my enthusiasm for life itself dwindled. The happy, outgoing, motivated woman I had previously been was gone. This new person was the complete opposite of the "real" me – unhappy, unmotivated, and unfulfilled. I lacked all the luster of my true personality and remained in this unconscious state for several years. I was a shell, simply existing My flatlined condition had targeted my mind, body, and spirit.

MY ROAD TO DISCOVERY & RECOVERY

I began to wake up every morning disgusted and lacking contentment in my life. The energetic, enthusiastic woman I used to be began to fade until I finally reached a point where I knew it was time for recovery. I was cheating my husband and my children of the empowered woman they deserved to have in their lives. More importantly, I was cheating myself of the empowered life I deserved, using my time to sulk and express disgust instead of devising a plan and creating the life I desired. As I began focusing on waking up out of my flatlined condition, I had to establish what the driving force was behind my state of depression and unhappiness, I had to get to the core of the problem. And I began to realize that my condition was not as simple as exhaustion or burnout from long days or lack of rest. It was much deeper. These feelings of unfulfillment and discontent centered around my desire for independence, freedom, and flexibility in my life and having control of my day-to-day schedule. My condition was primarily related to the fact that I wasn't living according to my true purpose. I had reached a crossroads in my life where I yearned for more – the need to be a part of something purposeful and meaningful. The time had come for me to discover my purpose and pursue my passion in life. So, I began taking baby steps towards creating the fulfillment I desired and deserved.

When I stepped out on faith and started taking control of my life, I began to see glimpses of recovery by means of discovery. My first step towards recovery was to implement a powerful change that would assist me in achieving all of my goals simultaneously – I stepped into entrepreneurship. Before I decided what business I would pursue I brainstormed on what was important to me, what could change and grow with me, what I would always enjoy doing, and what would demonstrate the fire and passion within. I took the time to read books, learn about numerous success stories of women who had changed their lives through entrepreneurship, and start networking with other positive, like-minded women who had already accomplished what I desired. I knew I possessed the talent, skills, determination, and focus to start my own business and to make it successful in an effort to create change in my life. I recognized that entrepreneurship could offer the potential for me to gain the complete freedom I was looking for -- financial freedom, freedom of time and schedule, freedom to prioritize my life the way I deemed fit, and freedom to live on purpose and with passion. Once I overcame my own doubts and fears and moved full speed ahead with the THING (for me, it was empowering other women and moms) that brought me the most joy in life, my small business, Moms R The Best, was born in June 2009. I quickly discovered that I had choices in life, that I could reclaim my independence and freedom, that I could pursue what I was passionate about, help others, and earn a living all at once, and I discovered that my destiny was completely in my control. Of course, as with any endeavor the what-ifs were lingering in the back of my mind but I knew I could never experience the life I wanted if I never put forth the effort. I owed it to myself, my husband, and my children to exert everything within me to create this life change.

By taking the leap of stepping into entrepreneurship, although I continued to work a full-time job, my eyes were opened to a world of fulfillment and inner joy because of the limitless opportunities I could create for myself while enjoying my passion. Not only did I step into my purpose but I began changing other's lives in the process. And as I reflect back, I often wonder why I didn't have the courage to take this step and embrace my God-given talents much sooner. As with so many who are reading this book, I possessed certain skills and talents, but I refused to embrace those skills and talents in order to live my best life. Perhaps it was a fear of failure, fear of success, or simply a fear of the responsibilities that come along with effecting change in other people's lives. But I began to see that nothing could replace the happiness that comes with stepping fully into your passion and purpose. Now, these many years after flatlining, I finally embrace my talent to empower, inspire, and motivate others as a speaker, motivational coach, workshop facilitator, and author. It is the THING I was meant to do, that I was created for, and I accept the responsibilities that come along with it. Fear no longer controls my life or paralyzes me into inactivity. Rather, I control my own destiny.

THE TRANSITION TO EMPOWERED LIVING

The only resolution for exiting my flatlined condition was to reach a subconscious level of joy, happiness and inner contentment, and then begin working on the actual reality. I had to change my mindset and focus on what I truly wanted to achieve in my life – my dreams, my goals, my aspirations, my ambitions. I had to dismiss all doubts and fears, overcome roadblocks, and develop the confidence within that I could change my life and accomplish anything I set my mind to do. Once I developed an optimistic mindset I never looked back. Everyday, I began celebrating who I was as a person, my natural talents, the skills I had developed in life, the characteristics I had refined, and the qualities I possessed. And that celebration continues to this day.

As I set out on a mission to fulfill my own destiny, I discovered my innate ability to empower, inspire, and motivate others, especially young girls, women and moms, to discover their purpose and passion, to overcome roadblocks to successful living, and to set high expectations for their lives. I began sharing my personal story of recovery through my 45-day empowerment guide that I devised and implemented based on how I desired to live my own life. Each day I implemented one empowerment tip towards living a more fulfilled, meaningful, and happy life. Now, I gladly share with you my 45-Day Guide to Empowered Living. As you build on each day of empowerment you will begin to feel refreshed, renewed, and reenergized to live your life with positivity, purpose, confidence, courage, tenacity, and boldness. Take advantage of the journaling page to the right of each empowerment tip to promote a deeper understanding of how the empowerment tip is transforming you into a new person. I recommend reading the daily tips at the start of your day as you are having your breakfast or morning coffee, before you step outside your door or start working on projects for the day. Allow the empowerment tips to penetrate your heart and to mold you into a person who sees life through glass eyes, with positivity, joy, and focus. As you journal each day be honest and forthright in your observation of your personal behavior, patterns, and thought processes, and determine how you can implement positive and progressive changes in your life. Focus on how each tip can help you to become a stronger, wiser, and happier person, family member, community member, and member of society.

I have also included two Reaffirmation Oaths at the conclusion of the 45-Day Guide To Empowered Living for you to repeat as often as necessary. The Reaffirmation Oaths will serve as reassurance that you have what it takes to reach for the stars and live the life you deserve. The oaths will provide empowerment and inspiration whether you are experiencing a day where you feel motivated, determined, and focused or if you are experiencing a day where you feel unmotivated, challenged, and unfocused. Continue to repeat the Reaffirmation Oaths to build confidence in your ability to change your life. Never forget that life is an experience and you should never let it pass you by. Starting today, join me as you become B.A.D. (Bold. Audacious. Determined.). You deserve it!

45-DAY GUIDE TO EMPOWERED LIVING

DAY 1 EMPOWERMENT TIP
BE CONFIDENT

CONFIDENCE is a state of mind characterized by belief in your abilities; a quality of being certain. Work hard to exude confidence in your life but beware of arrogance. Confidence is an inner assurance and belief that you WILL accomplish anything you set your mind to do, that you WILL succeed and make your life all that it is meant to be, that you WILL demand the best from yourself and those who enter your life, and that you WILL feel worthy of the best! Confidence is necessary for any goals in your life whether related to health, finances, relationships, career, education, or business endeavors.

DAILY JOURNALING

How did I implement this Empowerment Tip into my daily routine today? How will I use this tip in the future?

DAY 2 EMPOWERMENT TIP
STAY ENERGIZED

YOUR ENERGY is what draws or detracts people and opportunities to your life. Your personal energy can be positive and motivating or negative and draining. If your energy is positive, kind, and selfless you will attract the same to you. If your energy is pessimistic, unhappy, and empty that is what you will attract. Everyday work diligently to keep your energy levels full of enthusiasm, excitement, passion and appreciation for life, a desire to help others, and the motivation to be your very best. You deserve it.

Positive in, Positive out.

DAILY JOURNALING

How did I implement this Empowerment Tip into my daily routine today? How will I use this tip in the future?

DAY 3 EMPOWERMENT TIP
SEEK OPPORTUNITY

OPPORTUNITY sometimes only knocks once. When it knocks will you answer? Are you prepared for the knock or will you allow it to pass you by? Being prepared for opportunity involves doing your research and laying the foundation for the life goals you want to achieve, developing relationships with individuals who can assist opportunity in finding you, and exerting the effort to plant the seeds of success without fear of starting at the bottom and taking baby steps to work your way to the top.

DAILY JOURNALING

How did I implement this Empowerment Tip into my daily routine today? How will I use this tip in the future?

DAY 4 EMPOWERMENT TIP
THINK LIKE A LEADER

LEADERSHIP is an imperative skill for empowered living. Being a leader denotes focus, assertiveness, and determination in guiding your life towards the path you most desire. As a leader, you must forgo all timidity and approach life with boldness and audacity. Find the leadership skills within to take full control of your life and make a conscious decision to live up to your fullest potential, to think BIG and achieve BIG, and to continue setting new ceilings for yourself so that you always exceed even your own expectations.

DAILY JOURNALING

How did I implement this Empowerment Tip into my daily routine today? How will I use this tip in the future?

DAY 5 EMPOWERMENT TIP
ALWAYS KEEP A SMILE

SMILING alters your mood, relieves stress, boosts your immune system, puts you in a positive mind frame, and even makes you look younger. Avoid the habit of frowning even when life gets you down. The next time you feel stressed or bothered by life take a few minutes to reflect on all that you have to smile about. There is always a positive thought to outweigh a negative one. So focus on the positive and think about the many lives you brighten when you smile. Remember that smiling is contagious, so show the world your pearly whites on a daily basis.

DAILY JOURNALING

How did I implement this Empowerment Tip into my daily routine today? How will I use this tip in the future?

DAY 6 EMPOWERMENT TIP
SET EXPECTATIONS

EXPECTATIONS are key to how you live your life. What are your personal expectations for your life? If you have low or average expectations that is what your life will reflect. On the other hand, if you expect to soar to new heights, expect to think outside the box, expect to be creative, expect to live a life without drama, expect to have a positive and supportive inner circle, and expect to experience happiness, contentment, passion, and purpose that is what your life will reflect.

DAILY JOURNALING

How did I implement this Empowerment Tip into my daily routine today? How will I use this tip in the future?

DAY 7 EMPOWERMENT TIP
MAKE LASTING FIRST IMPRESSIONS

FIRST IMPRESSIONS are lasting impressions regardless of whether it is a face-to-face introduction or through social media. Your personal appearance (and photos you post on social media sites), your dialogue (and content of your social media posts), and your association (and friends on social media sites) tell others a lot about you. Always take time to do a self-evaluation and consider whether the impression you are leaving matches your intentions and the "real you". Implement changes where necessary. You only get one chance to make a first impression so make it a positively lasting one.

DAILY JOURNALING

How did I implement this Empowerment Tip into my daily routine today? How will I use this tip in the future?

DAY 8 EMPOWERMENT TIP
EXHIBIT PATIENCE

PATIENCE is a virtue worth developing and exhibiting in your daily life. Patience goes a long way in achieving the life you really want for yourself – patience to find a compatible life partner, to grow a successful business, to receive recognition on a job for an extraordinary accomplishment, to endure the challenge of rearing a child(ren) as a single parent, to experience financial growth, or to achieve a desired weight loss goal. Having the patience to be "still" in life and allow things to happen at the right time is sometimes the best course of action to become empowered.

DAILY JOURNALING

How did I implement this Empowerment Tip into my daily routine today? How will I use this tip in the future?

DAY 9 EMPOWERMENT TIP
BE OPTIMISTIC

OPTIMISM is a key ingredient to achieving success in any aspect of your life – finances, relationships, career or business, higher education, or health and wellness. Optimism entails developing a positive mindset and outlook on life, considering the glass to be half-full versus half-empty, turning odds into opportunities, demonstrating hopefulness and confidence regarding your future, and focusing on what you can learn from challenging situations. Are you living your life with optimism supported by positive actions?

DAILY JOURNALING

How did I implement this Empowerment Tip into my daily routine today? How will I use this tip in the future?

DAY 10 EMPOWERMENT TIP
TREAT YOUR BODY AS YOUR TEMPLE

YOUR BODY IS YOUR TEMPLE and must be loved and cared for. A crucial component of empowered living is self-care and nurturing of your mind, body, and soul. Because life is full of competing priorities and obligations you can quickly fall into a slump of feeling overwhelmed and on the verge of burnout. It is imperative that you demonstrate self-love and never take your body for granted. Make time for adequate rest, incorporate healthy eating and exercise into your daily routine, visit the doctor for regular, preventative appointments, and find ways to reduce stress in your life.

DAILY JOURNALING

How did I implement this Empowerment Tip into my daily routine today? How will I use this tip in the future?

DAY 11 EMPOWERMENT TIP
BE KIND

KINDNESS is free, yet, has become nearly obsolete in society as a whole. The great thing about kindness is that it can be displayed with words or actions – it is your choice. When was the last time you offered a kind word or smile to someone you did not know? When was the last time you were kind in offering assistance to a relative or friend in need? Displaying kindness on a daily basis will bring you happiness and inner joy beyond compare. I challenge you to demonstrate kindness to at least one person today.

DAILY JOURNALING

How did I implement this Empowerment Tip into my daily routine today? How will I use this tip in the future?

DAY 12 EMPOWERMENT TIP
DON'T BECOME COMPLACENT

COMPLACENCY can cause you to miss out on life. Avoid getting stuck in a rut and doing the same thing day-in and day-out with no real purpose. Remind yourself to come off of autopilot and LIVE life, not exist in life. Repeat the affirmation: "I will not become complacent in my life. I will be the very best that I can be. Nothing will stand in my way of accomplishing my goals. I will dream big. I will use every breath in my body and ounce of energy I have to make my life meaningful and purposeful. I will show appreciation and value for my life. Fears, doubts, and what-ifs will not stifle my progress.

DAILY JOURNALING

How did I implement this Empowerment Tip into my daily routine today? How will I use this tip in the future?

DAY 13 EMPOWERMENT TIP
PROVIDE SERVICE

SERVICE is a vital part of empowered living. Always view life from a standpoint of giving. Every individual has a responsibility to help guide or serve another person in some capacity. Each day presents a new opportunity for you to serve a small business by referring them to your network of contacts; volunteer your time, talents, or financial means to support a worthy organization in your community; or share your personal life story as a way to teach others. The more you give and serve the more you will receive!

DAILY JOURNALING

How did I implement this Empowerment Tip into my daily routine today? How will I use this tip in the future?

DAY 14 EMPOWERMENT TIP
BE OPEN TO CHANGE

CHANGE occurs in every aspect of life. Nothing stays the same and everything has its season. Never be afraid of change. Without it, you would not experience the joys of growth, progress, or achievement. And you would never experience the comeback from adversity, disappointment, or failure. The more you grow as a person you will likely experience change on a more consistent basis. Make a resolve to reflect on how change in your life makes you a better, more balanced and well-rounded person.

DAILY JOURNALING

How did I implement this Empowerment Tip into my daily routine today? How will I use this tip in the future?

DAY 15 EMPOWERMENT TIP
CHALLENGE YOURSELF

CHALLENGE YOURSELF everyday to become a better person. Challenge yourself to invest more time into your personal growth and development, to increase your level of service to others, to improve your self-confidence and self-awareness, to view the positive side of situations that come your way instead of the negative side, to venture out to do something new, to dream bigger than you have ever dreamed before, and to overcome roadblocks preventing you from stepping into your purpose.

DAILY JOURNALING

How did I implement this Empowerment Tip into my daily routine today? How will I use this tip in the future?

DAY 16 EMPOWERMENT TIP
ENVISION YOUR SUCCESS

SUCCESS is never achieved in the blink of an eye. Individuals who might appear to have achieved overnight success have usually been perfecting their craft for many years. You must remain determined, diligent, persistent, courageous, and fearless as you pursue your dreams and create your own destiny. Develop the mentality that failure is not an option. Never stop working towards your goals and dreams, always maintain belief in yourself and your abilities to achieve big. And if things get a little rocky in the interim just hold on and enjoy the ride.

DAILY JOURNALING

How did I implement this Empowerment Tip into my daily routine today? How will I use this tip in the future?

DAY 17 EMPOWERMENT TIP
LOVE YOURSELF

SELF-LOVE is mandatory for living an empowered life. You must love yourself for every positive and negative thing about you. Do you dislike a certain part of your body or possess some character flaw? Are you unhappy with your life status at the moment? Take a deep breath, exhale, and remember that every moment in life is precious… too precious to focus solely on what you dislike, on what you are not, or what you have not accomplished. And life is too short for regrets, so rather than dwell on the negative take time to regroup and refocus on implementing positive changes one small step at a time.

DAILY JOURNALING

How did I implement this Empowerment Tip into my daily routine today? How will I use this tip in the future?

DAY 18 EMPOWERMENT TIP
PERSEVERE

PERSEVERANCE is a must if you are going to succeed and overcome life's obstacles. Never, Never, Never Give Up! At times, life will come at you full speed ahead. You will not always know what the outcome of a challenging situation will be, but recognize that challenges build character and perseverance builds strength. You CAN persevere and endure any challenge in your life whether it involves your health, financial status, career progression, business endeavors, or family issues.

DAILY JOURNALING

How did I implement this Empowerment Tip into my daily routine today? How will I use this tip in the future?

DAY 19 EMPOWERMENT TIP
TAKE ACTION

ACTIONS speak louder than words; therefore, you must be a person who doesn't simply talk about life goals but who takes steps to achieve those goals. This must be applied in every aspect of your life. Do you have a goal of owning your own business? Do you have a desire to make a career change towards pursuing your passion and not just a paycheck? Do you want to achieve improved health and fitness? Do you want to give your finances an overhaul? Do you want to create positive, new relationships in your life? In order to achieve anything in your life you must always put your thoughts, ideas, goals, and dreams into motion.

DAILY JOURNALING

How did I implement this Empowerment Tip into my daily routine today? How will I use this tip in the future?

DAY 20 EMPOWERMENT TIP
LOOK FOR THE SILVER LINING

A SILVER LINING lies behind every cloud. Of course, it is difficult to express such assurance when you are experiencing a challenging situation in your life, but it is important to allow your inner strength, determination, and courage to shine through as you overcome challenges rather than allowing the challenges to consume you. Always focus on the knowledge that better days will come, that there is always someone who is experiencing a tougher hardship than you, and that the only way to grow as a person is to face challenges head-on with a positive attitude acknowledging that there is always a lesson to be learned.

DAILY JOURNALING

How did I implement this Empowerment Tip into my daily routine today? How will I use this tip in the future?

DAY 21 EMPOWERMENT TIP
USE TIME WISELY

TIME is irreplaceable. You can never go back to retrace your steps or get time back. Stop and ask yourself: How am I spending my time? Am I using it to accomplish what I really desire in my life? Am I living up to my fullest potential? Am I pursuing my passion and living with purpose? Am I using my time to give back to the community and help others? No one can turn back the hands of time so take full advantage of your time and LIVE BOLDLY! Never allow the fear of success, fear of failure, or fear of the unknown to prevent you from purposeful living.

DAILY JOURNALING

How did I implement this Empowerment Tip into my daily routine today? How will I use this tip in the future?

DAY 22 EMPOWERMENT TIP
MAINTAIN HAPPINESS

HAPPINESS in your life is completely in your control. You will never benefit if you complain about an unhappy life situation but don't work to make changes. Change is always difficult but imagine the results and joy on the other side of change. Come to the understanding that in order to LIVE life and not EXIST in life everything in your surroundings must celebrate you as a person and enhance your life rather than distract from your life. If you are unhappy with a life situation, take action and make changes. You deserve complete happiness.

DAILY JOURNALING

How did I implement this Empowerment Tip into my daily routine today? How will I use this tip in the future?

DAY 23 EMPOWERMENT TIP
CELEBRATE YOURSELF

CELEBRATE YOURSELF on a daily basis for all your wonderful qualities, characteristics, and gifts that you offer to the world. You have special gifts that you bring to the table and it is imperative that you use your gifts to better yourself and live the life you deserve. Take time everyday to celebrate something you love about your inner beauty and your outer beauty. Avoid all negative self talk. Confidently celebrate YOU and surround yourself with others who celebrate you. Remove all negativity, drama, and instability from your life and your inner circle.

DAILY JOURNALING

How did I implement this Empowerment Tip into my daily routine today? How will I use this tip in the future?

DAY 24 EMPOWERMENT TIP
CONTROL YOUR DESTINY

YOUR DESTINY lies in your hands. You cannot wait on anyone else to create the path to your destiny. Despite how great your passion or desire, there is never any guarantee that doors will be opened or opportunities presented. You must open your own doors and create your own opportunities to create your destiny. Be resourceful, be creative, be confident. And do not be afraid to start making progress towards your destiny in small steps. Anything worth having is worth putting in the hard work to achieve.

DAILY JOURNALING

How did I implement this Empowerment Tip into my daily routine today? How will I use this tip in the future?

DAY 25 EMPOWERMENT TIP
REVITALIZE

REVITALIZATION is imperative if you intend to live your best life. Amidst the hustle and bustle of your daily responsibilities you must take time to regroup, refresh, and reenergize your body and soul. Schedule a massage, treat yourself to a facia or pedicure, have dinner with a supportive group of friends take a long bath after you have completed a long day of work, read an empowering book or poem, or just sit at a local coffee shop and indulge while enjoying the serenity Your life is too precious to experience burn-out simply because you did not make time to revitalize.

DAILY JOURNALING

How did I implement this Empowerment Tip into my daily routine today? How will I use this tip in the future?

DAY 26 EMPOWERMENT TIP
PROTECT YOUR MENTAL HEALTH

YOUR MENTAL HEALTH is vital. As a busy member of society you have competing responsibilities and priorities to juggle on a daily basis. Even those who possess the greatest inner strength are not obsolete from experiencing feelings of worry, anxiety, sadness, or overload. Therefore, in caring for your mental health it is vital that you get adequate rest and relaxation, implement regular, physical exercise, develop a friendship with someone who is always willing to give you a listening ear, and make time for activities that bring you tranquility and fulfillment.

DAILY JOURNALING

How did I implement this Empowerment Tip into my daily routine today? How will I use this tip in the future?

DAY 27 EMPOWERMENT TIP
BE COURAGEOUS

COURAGE is crucial in your daily living as an empowered individual. Reaffirm to yourself: I have the courage to overcome any life obstacle; I have the courage to walk away from negative influences and unhealthy relationships; I have the courage to step out on faith and pursue my passion in life; I have the courage to fulfill my goals; I have the courage to pursue a higher education despite my fears; I have the courage to live the best life I can possibly live without regrets.

DAILY JOURNALING

How did I implement this Empowerment Tip into my daily routine today? How will I use this tip in the future?

DAY 28 EMPOWERMENT TIP
STAY FOCUSED

FOCUS is necessary to accomplish your life goals. Focus entails "intently directing your thoughts and efforts on a thing." Allow the passion for your goals and your drive to live your best life to keep you focused even in the face of doubts, fears, and minor setbacks. When you possess focus there is nothing that can stop you from achieving your goals no matter how big, small, or mediocre.

DAILY JOURNALING

How did I implement this Empowerment Tip into my daily routine today? How will I use this tip in the future?

DAY 29 EMPOWERMENT TIP
BE PREPARED

PREPARATION is vital to anything you want to accomplish in life. Whether you're planning to start your own business, change careers, pursue a higher education, enter a relationship, or build your wealth… you must prepare. Do your research, make a list of the pros and cons, talk to others who have experienced success in the area you are trying to achieve success, and always devise a "Plan B" with the mindset that you will never actually need it. Preparation almost always prevents failure.

DAILY JOURNALING

How did I implement this Empowerment Tip into my daily routine today? How will I use this tip in the future?

DAY 30 EMPOWERMENT TIP
INSPIRE OTHERS

INSPIRE OTHERS on a constant basis. When you have moments where you are feeling low with no where to turn, find a way to be an inspiration or a blessing to someone else. Find a way to take the focus off of yourself by lending a listening ear to someone who is having difficulty in their life, by performing a kind gesture for someone else in need, or by encouraging or inspiring a friend or family member who is lacking a strong support system. The more you exert yourself towards inspiring others the better you will feel about your personal situation.

DAILY JOURNALING

How did I implement this Empowerment Tip into my daily routine today? How will I use this tip in the future?

DAY 31 EMPOWERMENT TIP
LOVE WHAT YOU DO

LOVE WHAT YOU DO. Earning a living to care for everyday needs and to live the lifestyle you personally want to live is a necessity. However, if you don't love what you do you will still experience a void in your life. You will not have true happiness and contentment despite how much money you make. So, take the time to discover what you are passionate about, what brings you enjoyment, what makes you feel alive inside, and create the career you really want. When you do what you love it won't feel like a job at all. Don't exist aimlessly in life as though you don't have an option to create the life you really want.

DAILY JOURNALING

How did I implement this Empowerment Tip into my daily routine today? How will I use this tip in the future?

DAY 32 EMPOWERMENT TIP
GAIN STRENGTH

STRENGTH is built from life experiences. What doesn't break you will only make you stronger. In order to experience personal growth and build characteristics such as perseverance, boldness, determination, and fearlessness you must endure challenging, even difficult, situations in life. At times you will not understand why you are experiencing the challenge or how you will make it through. But when you hold your head up high and anticipate the joy that will result from enduring the challenge you will become stronger. Tap into your innermost strength and never allow any challenge to break your spirit for more than 60 seconds.

DAILY JOURNALING

How did I implement this Empowerment Tip into my daily routine today? How will I use this tip in the future?

DAY 33 EMPOWERMENT TIP
DISCOVER YOUR PURPOSE

PURPOSE can be discovered by focusing on the capacity in which you can best serve others. What brings you the utmost joy in life, especially as you affect others lives in a positive and empowered way? Stepping into your life purpose will result in a satisfaction, fulfillment, and contentment that is incomparable. Take the time to discover what your true purpose or calling in life is and devote one hundred percent into living it.

DAILY JOURNALING

How did I implement this Empowerment Tip into my daily routine today? How will I use this tip in the future?

DAY 34 EMPOWERMENT TIP
FIND YOUR PASSION

PASSION is the fuel that fires the best person within. To live the most fulfilling and rewarding life, take time to discover your passion and then allow that passion to surface and display itself. When you make the determination to pursue your passion you will not allow anything to stop you from living your best life. You will possess the faith and confidence that YOU CAN do anything you set out to do. No mountain, regardless of how tall or steep, will prevent you from reaching the top.

DAILY JOURNALING

How did I implement this Empowerment Tip into my daily routine today? How will I use this tip in the future?

DAY 35 EMPOWERMENT TIP
RESPECT YOURSELF

RESPECT denotes a positive feeling of esteem for a person. However, respect starts with self. Do you have a deep respect for yourself? Is it displayed in the way you carry yourself? Your language? The way your inner circle treats you? If you do not respect yourself noone else will believe you are worthy of respect. By the same token, you must give respect to get respect.

DAILY JOURNALING

How did I implement this Empowerment Tip into my daily routine today? How will I use this tip in the future?

DAY 36 EMPOWERMENT TIP
BE HUMBLE

Allow HUMILITY to be a part of your everyday character. When you demonstrate humility there is no room for arrogance, pride, or exalting yourself above others regardless of your status or success in life. Always look for ways to "serve" others including family, friends, community members, and even strangers. Humility is a quality that attracts positive energy to your life, so demonstrate it frequently.

DAILY JOURNALING

How did I implement this Empowerment Tip into my daily routine today? How will I use this tip in the future?

DAY 37 EMPOWERMENT TIP
DEVELOP YOUR CORE STRENGTHS

DEVELOP YOUR CORE STRENGTHS in your pursuit of living an empowered life. If you have strength motivating others find ways to develop that core strength by getting involved in local groups that effect change in your community. If you have strength connecting people, develop that core strength by helping local business owners build relationships and create opportunities with each other. Developing your core strengths will benefit you and those whose lives you touch with your special gifts.

DAILY JOURNALING

How did I implement this Empowerment Tip into my daily routine today? How will I use this tip in the future?

DAY 38 EMPOWERMENT TIP MONITOR YOUR PERSONAL GROWTH

PERSONAL GROWTH is an important area of focus in your life. Making your personal growth and development a priority is essential. It involves opening your mind and being willing to explore new thoughts, ideas, experiences, opportunities and concepts. Personal growth results from a combination of successes, failures, and attempts. With each, you succeed because the lessons learned are irreplaceable. What steps are you taking towards nurturing your personal growth and development?

DAILY JOURNALING

How did I implement this Empowerment Tip into my daily routine today? How will I use this tip in the future?

DAY 39 EMPOWERMENT TIP
STAY IN YOUR LANE

YOUR LANE in life is determined by your actions. Are you in the fast lane of doers or in the slow lane of talkers who take no action to live the life they deserve? If you intend to reach your dreams, achieve higher heights, and live a life of purpose, fulfillment, and success you must be a doer. Take steps today to develop a blueprint for your life, surround yourself with individuals who can and want to help you fulfill your blueprint, and avoid procrastinating on implementing your blueprint. A big part of experiencing life is taking chances and pursuing what may seem impossible.

DAILY JOURNALING

How did I implement this Empowerment Tip into my daily routine today? How will I use this tip in the future?

DAY 40 EMPOWERMENT TIP
RISE UP

RISE UP and live your life with confidence, boldness, fearlessness, and courage. Are you tired of simply existing, not understanding your purpose, going about a daily routine with no real focus or goals. In order to reach your full potential in life you must not exist with fear, timidity, or low self-confidence. Rise up, hold your head up high, and discover the strong, bold, determined person inside. Constantly feed your mind positive thoughts, be sure that your inner circle supports and motivates you to be a better person, and reassure yourself that you deserve successful living.

DAILY JOURNALING

How did I implement this Empowerment Tip into my daily routine today? How will I use this tip in the future?

DAY 41 EMPOWERMENT TIP
REACH FOR THE SKY

THE SKY IS THE LIMIT so get creative and think outside the box when it comes to living your life to its fullest. Do not allow yourself to fall into a rut where you feel you have to follow the "norm" and live according to what everyone else does. Set your own boundaries and dream big. Rather than allowing life to become a routine, make it an experience. Be resourceful and find ways to continually challenge yourself to do better, to become better, and to feel better about your life journey.

DAILY JOURNALING

How did I implement this Empowerment Tip into my daily routine today? How will I use this tip in the future?

DAY 42 EMPOWERMENT TIP
HAVE A POSITIVE MINDSET

POSITIVE MINDSET must accompany anything you do in your life. Any goal you want to achieve, any dream you want to reach requires a mental toughness and consistency. You must maintain a positive, confident, and forward-thinking mindset in order to achieve BIG. Never allow negative thinking, doubts, fears, what-ifs, or setbacks to hinder you from pursue a life of empowerment.

DAILY JOURNALING

How did I implement this Empowerment Tip into my daily routine today? How will I use this tip in the future?

DAY 43 EMPOWERMENT TIP
STAY GROUNDED

STAY GROUNDED in your life no matter how great your achievements or accomplishments. It is crucial that you make time to reflect on the fact that true purpose and contentment is found in using your talents and "status" to help someone else, to bring attention to important issues in your community, to give back to those less fortunate, and to create valuable opportunities to help others achieve success. Surrounding yourself with those who understand the act of giving and the power of service is one sure way to stay grounded as well as finding ways to donate your time, energy, and resources to supporting worthy causes.

DAILY JOURNALING

How did I implement this Empowerment Tip into my daily routine today? How will I use this tip in the future?

DAY 44 EMPOWERMENT TIP
SLOW DOWN & SMELL THE ROSES

SLOW DOWN and SMELL THE ROSES. Like most, you probably find your life on wharp-speed, constantly on the go, handling everyday necessities, running errands, closing deals in the boardroom, networking and brainstorming on new concepts for your business, spending quality time with your family, and more. But make the determination today to marvel at the sunset, enjoy the cool breeze, smell some beautiful flowers, or enjoy a scoop of ice cream. It's the little wonders in life that can help you to fully develop a spirit of gratitude and enhance empowered living. Don't let life pass you by.

DAILY JOURNALING

How did I implement this Empowerment Tip into my daily routine today? How will I use this tip in the future?

DAY 45 EMPOWERMENT TIP
BE APPRECIATIVE

A deep APPRECIATION for all that your life can be is vital to empowered living. Appreciate each morning you wake up to breath, live, and experience another day in making strides towards what you really want your life to look like; Appreciate the talent and skills you possess; Appreciate that life's challenges will only make you stronger and build character if you allow it to; Appreciate that you have choices in life and can take full control of your destiny.

DAILY JOURNALING

How did I implement this Empowerment Tip into my daily routine today? How will I use this tip in the future?

REAFFIRMATION OATH 1

I am talented and gifted
I am creative and resourceful
I will remain determined to live successfully
I will stay focused on my life goals
I will be courageous in my life journey

I will never allow my doubts
I will never allow my fears
I will never allow negative thinking
I will never allow minor setbacks
To stand in my way

I will surround myself with those who support my growth
I will surround myself with those who hold me accountable
I will surround myself with those who want to see me succeed

Success belongs to me
I own it, I believe it, I will achieve it
I possess the strength within
I possess the perseverance
I possess the determination
I possess the confidence
To live my BEST life!

REAFFIRMATION OATH 2

I have what it takes to be anything I want to be
I am strong, I am confident, I am bold
My courage and determination are shining thru

I will go after my dreams
I will be my very best
I will live up to my fullest potential

I will step into my purpose
I will pursue my passion
I will celebrate my accomplishments
I will be inspired by my achievements
I will learn from my failures
I will continue to grow in every step I take in life

I will become the empowered person I am destined to be!

CONCLUSION

Reflecting on the transformation that occurred in my life simply by taking action, I realize the only obstacle that ever stood in the way of me fulfilling my destiny was my own fear and lack of confidence to pursue and achieve my dreams. Likewise, you possess the ability to alter your life as you see fit. Create a roadmap of what your life currently looks like and then create a roadmap of the road you want to be on. Take the step of applying action to your thoughts, ideas, goals, and dreams. Don't allow stress, frustration, or lack of fulfillment to control your life. Replace all negative feelings with passion, purpose, positive energy, contentment, and fulfillment in your life. In a world of instant gratification you still have the option to slow down and take the time to discover who you really are, what makes you happy, and what fuels the fire within. Stop ignoring opportunities to live your best life now. Make a determination to come off of autopilot, take a look around you, recognize life, appreciate life, and stop existing. Come out of your flatlined condition today and take life by the reigns in order to see your heart fully beating again.

Breinigsville, PA USA
20 February 2011
255927BV00003B/7/P

9 781604 587333